SEALS

First published in Great Britain in 1991 by
Colin Baxter Photography Ltd.,
Unit 2/3, Block 6,
Caldwellside Industrial Estate,
LANARK, ML11 6SR

British Library Cataloguing in Publication Data
Miller, David
  Seals
  I. Seals (Mammals)
  I. Title
  599.745

  ISBN 0-948661-24-0

Photographs by

Front Cover © Laurie Campbell
Back Cover © Jane Burton (Bruce Coleman)
Page 19 © Tony Wharton (Frank Lane)
Page 20 © Leonard Lee Rue III (Bruce Coleman)
Page 21 © David Miller
Page 22 © Tony Wharton (Frank Lane)
Page 23 © Paul Thompson
Page 24 © Tony Wharton (Frank Lane)
Page 25 © Colin Baxter
Page 26 © George MacCarthy (Bruce Coleman)
Page 27 © Tony Wharton (Frank Lane)
Page 28 © David Miller
Page 29 © Jane Burton (Bruce Coleman)
Page 30 © Dr. Eckart Pott (Bruce Coleman)

Page 35 © Colin Baxter
Page 36 © J. V. & G. R. Harrison (Aquila)
Page 37 © Jeff Foott (Bruce Coleman)
Page 38 © Paul Thompson
Page 39 © Jeff Foott (Bruce Coleman)
Page 40 © Nigel Dennis (NHPA)
Page 41 © Paul Thompson
Page 42 (Top) © Paul Thompson
Page 42 (Bottom) © Doug Allan (Oxford Scientific Films)
Page 43 © Jeff Foott (Survival Anglia)
Page 44 © Laurie Campbell (NHPA)
Page 45 © David Doubilet
Page 46 © Jim Bain (NHPA)

Seal Illustration © Keith Brockie

Printed in Great Britain by
Frank Peters (Printers) Ltd., Kendal.

SEALS

David Miller

Colin Baxter Photography Ltd., Lanark, Scotland

Seals

Seals are among our most immediately recognisable and best loved wild animals. This is perhaps surprising because they spend most of their lives at sea, out of the sight of man, and come ashore mainly on the more remote parts of our densely populated islands. Indeed, there are probably many people who have never actually seen one in the wild. Among those who have, there can be few who were not captivated by the inquisitive dog-like face breaking the surface of the water.

It is paradoxical therefore, that few animals provoke such extreme public opinion. Seals are seen on the one hand as cute, cuddly toys and on the other as marauding, voracious predators. These images are perpetuated by scenes of helpless pups clubbed to death on blood-covered ice, and by misleading claims of the damage done by seals to fish stocks. This image is further complicated by man's long involvement with seals, using them both as a resource and as the basis of traditional folklore. In 'selkie' stories of old, seals were once human children condemned to a life between land and sea, while in some places fishermen consider it unlucky to kill seals because they embody the souls of dead sailors.

Much of this superstition and ignorance results from the fact that seals are undoubtedly fascinating and enigmatic creatures and that they live in an environment which is alien to us. It is only in recent times that we have been able to explore the lives of seals in their own world and we are now beginning to unravel the mysteries of their lives beneath the ocean waves.

Seals belong to a group of mammals related to the carnivores (bears, dogs, cats and weasels) and called the Pinnipedia or 'flap-footed' animals after their large flippers. These pinnipeds are further divided into three families: the 'earless' seals (Phocidae), the 'eared' seals (Otariidae) and the walrus (Odobenidae). The 'seal' many people have seen in zoos and circuses, balancing balls and clapping with its fore-flippers, is, in fact, a Californian sea lion - an animal more at home in the surf of the distant Pacific. It belongs to the family Otariidae which comprises 15 species worldwide but with no representatives around the coasts of the British Isles. These 'eared seals' are only distantly related to the 'true' seals or Phocidae, which comprises 19 species worldwide and includes our own common seal and grey seal.

The origins of seals are shrouded in mystery as the earliest fossil records from some 20 million years ago reveal seals very much like those alive today. Other evidence suggests that the sea lions, fur seals and walruses may have evolved from a bear-like ancestor on the shores of the Pacific, while the Phocids arose more recently from an otter-like ancestor around the Atlantic. The constraints of life in the water have resulted in these two separate groups developing a remarkably similar stream-lined body shape and physiology through the process known as convergent evolution. Even so, they have retained important differences which make it relatively easy to tell them apart.

Among the most obvious of these are that sea lions and fur seals have external ear flaps, larger fore-flippers to propel themselves underwater, and hind-flippers which can turn forward, allowing them to stand on 'all-fours' and walk on land. Phocids, on the other hand, have no external ear flaps, they have relatively small fore-flippers and large hind-flippers which are their main form of propulsion underwater and which cannot be turned forward, with the result that phocids on land use an apparently awkward shuffling movement. Walruses, with their enormously enlarged upper canine teeth, have some of the characteristics of both groups and are in a family by themselves.

Although life in the water has dictated that seals resemble one another in shape, they are still a diverse group in many respects. For example, they range from the Arctic, where ringed seals have been recorded at the North Pole, down through the oceans of the world, to the Antarctic mainland where Weddell seals breed. Indeed, not all seals live in the sea. The world's largest freshwater body, Lake Baikal in the Soviet Union, supports a population of seals over 1,000 miles from the nearest ocean. Common seals are found in land-locked lakes in Canada, and in Britain they make forays up rivers, some even reaching Loch Ness, which perhaps explains a few monster sightings.

Seals vary greatly in size. The female Galapagos fur seal is among the smallest and measures 1.5 metres long and weighs around 35 kg. These adults are smaller than even a new-born pup of the gargantuan southern elephant seal, where adult males may reach 5 metres in length and weigh over 3.5 tonnes.

Seals also differ in their food preferences and while most are fish-eaters, some include cephalapods (squid and octopus) in their diet and a few specialise in other prey. For instance, the misnamed crabeater seal in Antarctica feeds on small shrimp-like crustaceans known as krill while the more aptly named leopard seal, with its formidable teeth, includes penguins and even the young of other seals in its diet.

All seals are stream-lined and have large flippers acting as paddles and rudders for efficient swimming underwater, which is essential for both catching prey and escaping from predators. However, to live successfully in the water these in themselves are not enough. As air-breathing, warm-blooded mammals they have made other important adaptations.

Water is a more efficient conductor of heat than air and since water temperatures are always lower than normal mammalian blood, seals have developed ingenious mechanisms for reducing heat loss. These have become so efficient that seals live in polar waters cold enough to kill an unprotected human diver in minutes. It is no coincidence that seals are large animals with a cylindrical shape and few appendages. This not only aids swimming, it provides a large inner volume where heat is maintained and a small surface area where it is lost.

They have also developed methods of insulation to reduce heat loss even further. The most obvious of these is the thick fur coat which is most advanced in the appropriately named fur seals. They have a particularly dense water-repellent undercoat which prevents water reaching the skin and is much sought after by hunters. However, fur has major drawbacks for a diving animal, because as depth increases, water pressure eliminates trapped air and compresses the fur, reducing its heat retaining properties. Seals have therefore developed another type of insulation, the special layer of fat known as blubber. This lies beneath the skin and cannot be compressed and so retains its value as an insulator at whatever depth a seal dives. This layer of blubber covers the body of the seal and may reach 10cm in thickness on seals which inhabit polar waters and it is this blubber which enables Weddell seals to tolerate temperatures as low as -40°C while hauled-out on ice. Common and grey seals in warmer, temperate waters have typical blubber thicknesses of up to 6cm.

Marine mammals must be able to dive efficiently, and for this seals have developed some quite remarkable adaptations. The simplest of these include the muscular reflex which closes the nostrils as a seal submerges, and the ability to close larynx and oesophagus when opening their mouths underwater. In order to dive as deep as their prey and spend time chasing and catching it, seals must also be able to hold their breath for extended periods. Although grey and common seals normally dive for around five minutes at a time, these dives can be repeated one after another with only short surface intervals for many hours. They are also capable of making much longer dives, up to about 30 minutes, and a Weddell seal has been known to make a dive lasting a remarkable 73 minutes.

Seals do not breathe in before they dive, as we would do. Taking down large volumes of air in their lungs would create difficulties with buoyancy and could lead to the 'bends' as they re-surfaced, a potentially fatal condition which affects human divers and is caused by nitrogen forming bubbles in blood. Seals avoid these problems and achieve astonishing diving feats by breathing out as they dive and carry the oxygen they need combined to special pigments in their blood and muscle tissue. Seals have more blood for their body size than any other mammal and it contains more of the oxygen-carrying pigment haemoglobin than ours and as much as 10 times the amount of oxygen-carrying myoglobin in the muscles.

But even this is only part of the story - as well as increasing the amount of oxygen they store, seals also use it in the most economical way. While diving they can reduce their heart rate to 4 or 5 beats per minute or about 10-20% of the pre-dive rate, a process known as bradycardia. This, combined with the ability to divert blood away from areas of the body where it is not needed (eg. the liver and kidneys) and to send it to essential organs, especially the brain, allows seals to survive very much longer dives than they would normally make.

Long dives may also mean deep dives and some seals are capable of reaching phenomenal depths. Common and grey seals in British waters are thought to feed near the seabed and are restricted to depths of around 50m in the waters in which they have been studied. From elsewhere it is known that they can reach depths of 100m but they have a long way to go to reach the champions of the seal diving world. Weddell seals have been shown to be capable of diving to 600m under the Antarctic ice and even this astonishing figure has recently been exceeded by northern elephant seals which dive to depths in excess of 1,000m in the Pacific.

Our knowledge of seal movements in and beneath the seas was very patchy until the 1970s when scientists began to develop recording instruments which could be harmlessly attached to seals and recovered later. Before these developments almost all information on seals was obtained from observations on land, mainly during the breeding season, or from dead animals drowned in fishing nets or killed by hunters. Today there are various instruments in use. These include time-depth recorders which give a print-out of the depths to which a seal has dived, and sonic transmitters used to track seals underwater from boats equipped with hydrophones, thus establishing the shape of a dive as well as its depth and duration. VHF radio transmitters are also used to track the movements of seals and because their signal can only be received when the seal is at the water's surface or on land, they can be used to compare the amount of time seals spend in the water as opposed to hauled-out. These VHF transmitters are as small as possible and have an effective range of only 20km which makes them less than ideal for tracking long offshore journeys. Exciting new technology has led to the development of UHF transmitters which can beam information up to passing satellites. It should soon be possible for scientists to track seals, in any of the world's oceans, from the comfort of their laboratories. Using techniques such as these, much has been learnt in the 1980s about the only two species of seal commonly found in British waters; the common seal and the grey seal.

The common seal, or harbour seal as it is known throughout the rest of the English-speaking world, is the most widespread of all seals. It is found on both sides of the north Atlantic, in the Arctic and around the rim of the north Pacific and has a world population estimated at 500,000. Paradoxically it is the less common of our seals with a UK population of around 25,000. The grey seal is found only in the north Atlantic and with a world population estimated at 200,000 it is less common in global terms than the common seal. However, in Britain there are over 90,000 grey seals which represent more than 90% of the western Atlantic population, making ours the single most important population. It follows therefore that we have a crucial, moral responsibility to protect these animals and the seas in which they live. Visitors to Britain from many European countries are enthralled and captivated by our seals, for in several cases theirs have been lost through persecution, pollution and disturbance.

Both species of seal are widespread around the British coast but they are particularly abundant in north and west Scotland. Grey seals congregate once a year to breed on rugged, uninhabited islands. The largest of these colonies are on North Rona and the Monach Isles in the Outer Hebrides, with other important concentrations in Orkney and Shetland and the largest in England at the Farne Islands off the Northumbrian coast. Grey seals are in general more widely distributed during the rest of the year when they are not breeding. Common seals are found on both rocky west coast shores and in some of the large estuaries on the east coast such as the Moray Firth and the Wash. They tend to live all year round in the same areas and are able to utilise more disturbed mainland sites than greys and can often be seen hauled-out, sometimes in large numbers, close to areas of human activity. Although grey seals breed in small numbers in Wales and south-west England, common seals are only occasionally seen and they do not breed south of the Thames in the east or south of the Clyde on the west. There are small populations of both species in Ireland.

It is clear then, that in many parts of their range grey and common seals occur together. So how can we tell them apart? This is not always easy and even experienced observers make mistakes. A small, dog-like head bobbing in the water is most likely a seal, although it may be an otter if very small. If only the head can be seen then its shape and the pattern of the nostrils are the best guide to identifying which type. If the animal is hauled-out, then size, coat pattern and colour should make things easier. In fact, reliable identification is often only possible using a combination of several features.

Grey seals are much the larger of the two and they are, in fact, the largest British mammal. Red deer are often quoted as our largest animals but Scottish stags weigh on average only 100kg compared with the average 230kg for a bull grey seal and some giants may exceed 350kg. Adult male grey seals are about 2m long and are both larger and heavier than females which may typically reach 180cm in length and 150kg in weight. So, although only slightly longer than females, males are very much heavier. This is reflected in their physique, with males having larger heads and much thicker necks. Common seals on the other hand are smaller animals which show little sexual dimorphism, that is, only a slight difference in size between sexes. Male common seals are only marginally larger on average than females and both may weigh between 80 and 100kg and measure 175cm in length.

Difference in size, however, is not usually much help in identification if all you can see is a head in the water. With a good view at short range and with some practice it is not too difficult. Grey seals have a much flatter head with a longer, pronounced 'Roman' nose whereas common seals have a more dog-like face with a shorter muzzle and steeper forehead - generally considered to be prettier. Pretty is not an adjective readily applied to a bull grey seal! Young grey seals pose more of a problem, they may be the same size as an adult common and may not have developed the pronounced 'Roman' nose but even these when seen from the front at close range can be distinguished, as the nostrils of a grey seal form almost parallel, vertical slits while those of a common form a V-shape.

When seals are hauled-out, coat colour and pattern can be useful for identification. Despite their name, grey seals, especially females, are widely variable in colour and range from pale grey or brown with almost no spots, through grey or brown with large black splodges, to almost black all over. Common seals can also be predominantly grey or brown but they are generally covered in small dark spots rather than the larger, more widely spaced blotches of the grey. There are, however, times of the year when coat colour and pattern cannot be used reliably for identification - this is during the moult when both species may become uniformly brown and their spots obscured.

Although seals are superbly adapted to life in the sea, unlike whales and dolphins there are aspects of their life cycle which require them to come ashore. The annual moult is such a time. In commons this happens about one month after the breeding season and in greys three to four months after breeding. At this time of the year some seals spend a particularly large amount of time ashore, but the reasons for this are not entirely clear. The most likely explanation is that by staying ashore they minimise heat loss and maintain a high skin temperature which accelerates the moulting process. Seals also spend varying amounts of time hauled-out at other times of year but the reasons are even more unclear. Contrary to popular belief they are not always basking in the sun because they haul-out even on bitterly cold winter days.

However, the prime reason for coming ashore during the annual cycle for all seals is the need to breed on land (or ice). In this they differ fundamentally from the whales and dolphins which mate, give birth and suckle their young underwater. Despite the fact that some seals mate in the water they all come ashore to give birth and to suckle their young, although this period of suckling may be incredibly short. The shortest of any mammal belongs to that of the female hooded seal on the Arctic pack ice who suckles her pup for only 4 days. Such short lactation times and correspondingly high pup growth rates are only possible because seal milk is the richest of any mammal's and has a consistency which has been described as more like mayonnaise than milk. Indeed seal milk may contain 60% fat and 10% protein compared with values of 3.5% fat and 1% protein for human milk.

Grey and common seals differ markedly in their breeding strategies. In the UK, grey seals pup in the autumn but the exact timing varies considerably from place to place. Breeding begins in September in Wales and south-west England, in September/October on the west coast of Scotland and not until November on the east coast of Scotland and north England. Females gather, often in very large numbers, at traditional breeding sites which are usually remote, uninhabited islands. They come ashore before giving birth and in complete contrast to common seals remain on land for the three weeks it takes to wean their pups. When born the pups weigh about 14kg and are covered in a thick white coat which provides insulation on land but becomes waterlogged if the pup enters the sea. The pups grow rapidly and at the end of the lactation period which lasts only about 18 days they will have trebled in weight. Conversely the mothers, who do not re-enter the water or feed at this time, may lose over one third of their body weight. The pups are then abandoned, lose their white coats and must learn to fend for themselves.

Meanwhile the females, once lactation has finished, become sexually receptive and mate with a nearby male. Male grey seals come ashore when the females are pupping and during lactation they use their large body size to fight and establish dominance relationships. The dominant males will then defend harems of 2-10 females against other males. Large size is important to male grey seals, not only because it enables them to win fights, it also allows them to spend a long time ashore without feeding. Whereas male grey seals may weigh two to three times as much as a female, male and female common seals are similar in size. This suggests that male common seals have a different mating strategy in which size is not so important.

Unlike grey seals the timing of common seal breeding is consistent around the British coast and begins in mid-June when females come ashore on intertidal sandbanks or rocks and give birth to their pups. Although small (10kg) and vulnerable when first born they are more advanced at this stage than most other types of seal pups. They have already shed their first white coat, or lanugo, in their mother's uterus and are able to swim and dive within the first hour. At this tender age they are, in fact, the best adapted of all seals to their watery environment and it is this which enables common seals to breed in areas disturbed by humans while grey seals are more restricted in their choice of breeding sites. Lactation lasts for 3-4 weeks during which time the pup more than doubles its weight on the rich milk. In the early stages, mother and pup remain close together and tend to haul-out at each low tide. The females probably spend little time feeding and may lose considerable weight. As weaning approaches the mothers make longer feeding trips but it is unclear whether pups accompany them or wait for their return. After weaning the pup must fend for itself, surviving on its blubber reserves until it is able to catch its own prey. Like grey seals, females become sexually receptive at the end of lactation but in contrast to most other seals mating takes place in the water and has rarely been observed. In both species a 2-3 month period of delayed implantation then follows before the development of the egg continues. This mechanism allows pups to be born at the same time every year despite the fact that gestation time is only 9 months. During the rest of the year females feed intensively, building up their blubber layer, to provide the fat reserves necessary for breeding next season.

Apart from the need to breed and moult on land, seals are supremely adapted to their marine environment. They can dive to great depths and remain underwater for long periods of time, and it is these very adaptations which enable them to exploit the food resources of the sea but which also make it so difficult to study. Early diet research was based largely on the stomach contents of seals shot near fishing nets. Not surprisingly these seals were eating the types of fish caught in the net, usually salmon. More recent research using less biased techniques reveals that British seals eat a variety of fish including sand eels, flatfish, cod, herring, and salmon as well as some cephalopods and crustaceans.

These techniques involve the identification of hard parts, particularly distinctive fish ear bones known as otoliths, from the stomach contents of seals killed away from fishing nets, or from their droppings at haul-out sites. There are, of course, also biases with these techniques. For instance, if seals do not eat the head of a particular species as has been suggested for salmon then otoliths will not be found; small otoliths may be digested completely, and haul-out site samples may not be representative of fish caught at sea.

Meanwhile, there is growing pressure from the fishing industry to provide answers to questions about what seals eat, where they feed and how much they eat. Scientists are beginning to answer the first two questions but how much seals eat and indeed how they catch their prey is more difficult to assess and depends on factors which cannot be measured at the present time. Even so, the general picture seems to be that British seals are opportunistic feeders who vary their food intake to include locally abundant prey and these may change from season to season, place to place and even year to year.

Common seals have a speckled coat and an attractive dog-like face.

This female grey seal, hauled-out on a breeding beach, has a flatter head
than a common seal. In male grey seals the characteristic
'Roman' nose is even more pronounced.

Throughout the year common seals *(above)* haul-out on intertidal sandbanks and rocks. They will often remain ashore for several hours, only returning to the water when the incoming tide washes them off their resting places.

In the autumn, grey seals gather at their traditional breeding sites on
remote, uninhabited islands such as Haaf Gruney in Shetland *(right)*.
The males *(above)* come ashore before the female and they
fight with one another to establish territories.

The difference in body size and head shape can be seen as these
male and female grey seals exchange threats on a breeding
beach *(above)*. The females take some time to choose a
suitable site to give birth to their pups *(left)*.

Most female grey seals remain ashore for three weeks and feed their
white-coated pups on fat-rich milk. Some pups, however, are
abandoned by their mothers and do not survive *(right)*.

Conservation of Seals

Interest in seals in Britain probably reached a peak during the phocine distemper virus (PDV) or 'seal plague' outbreak in 1988. The disease affected both species but particularly common seals with some 18,000 dying in Europe, 3,000 of them around the British Isles. Much scientific and media interest surrounded the epidemic and although a previously unidentified virus was discovered to be ultimately responsible, many aspects of the disease are not fully understood. It appears to have been the natural occurrence of a type of disease which has affected other seals in other places, and which may have affected British seals in the past. So, although in this case a man-made calamity was probably not responsible, the massive public interest highlighted the concern people have about the abuse of our oceans. Over-fishing, sewage discharge, oil pollution and waste disposal are just some of the threats facing seals and other marine life today.

Although nature conservation is a relatively recent phenomenon, man has been concerned with seals for a very long time. In fact, seal remains have been found in archaeological sites dating back to Neolithic times and it seems likely that seals would have fallen victim to the earliest hunter-gatherers as they followed the retreating ice some 10,000 years ago. A seal would have been a valuable quarry, being large, vulnerable on land, and providing meat for food, blubber for fuel and skins for clothing and shelter. Indeed, in the Arctic, the survival of the Inuit peoples was dependent on seals and seal products. Perhaps we should regard them, along with the North American Indians and their reliance on buffalo, as the original nature conservationists – people who viewed the environment with respect and had the sense to use its resources in a sustainable way. This type of subsistence hunting made relatively little impact on seal populations but everything changed with the advent of hunting for trade in the 18th century. Along with the great whales, many species of seal were exploited on a vast scale by hunters from Europe and North America. Perhaps as many as 2.5 million northern fur seals were slaughtered off Alaska, and northern elephant seals were reduced to a world population of less than 100 by 1890. Due to legal protection the populations of both species have since recovered and happily no longer face extinction.

Seal hunting around the British Isles never occurred on such a huge scale but even so it was sufficient to reduce the grey seal population to a reported 500 individuals in 1914. This led to the Grey Seal Protection Act (1914), the first time a British mammal (other than a game animal) had been protected by law. The hunting of common seals for their fur continued until the 1960s and the introduction of the Conservation of Seals Act (1970). Despite this hunting, seals in British waters have, in general, done rather well this century and the large increase in grey seals has brought them into conflict with fishermen.

The direct effects of seals on fishing nets and the fish within them are an age-old problem at salmon netting stations and more recently at fish farms, where nets are fixed and which seals associate with an abundant food supply. Despite protection, the law allows seals to be shot at or close to fishing gear and such shooting is likely to increase as both seals and fish farms increase. While many people argue that seals should be completely protected, it is undeniable that seal damage causes some fishermen great financial loss and seals themselves do not appear to be declining at this level of persecution. However, a wholesale reduction of seal numbers, as has been suggested by fishing interests, is morally unacceptable to most people and there is no scientific evidence to suggest it would reduce levels of damage. It is surely better to concentrate resources and research on developing and employing effective anti-predator nets or acoustic scaring devices.

Seals also affect fisheries indirectly by eating fish in the open sea which man could otherwise catch. While it is true that 92,000 grey and 25,000 common seals eat a great many fish there is little evidence to suggest that reducing seal numbers would increase the fish caught by commercial fisheries. In fact one could turn the argument around and suggest that over-fishing by man is reducing fish available to seals and other marine predators. This is just the situation which may have caused the decline of sand eels in Shetland and the subsequent collapse of seabird breeding success. Seals, however, are showing no signs of suffering from man's over-fishing; it seems they are more adaptable than Arctic terns or puffins and are able to switch if necessary to another food source. They are also better at catching fish than man!

As with so many things, we simply do not know enough about the marine ecosystem to blame seals for problems which we ourselves may have created. Indeed, seals are themselves killed in fishing nets, and die lingering deaths entangled in discarded waste. And there are other, more insidious, man-made threats.

Crude oil is the most conspicuous form of marine pollution and causes enormous damage to marine life, particularly seabirds as they rely on their feathers for insulation. The effects on seals are less dramatic because, unlike seabirds, they do not preen and ingest the oil so readily. They also rely on their blubber rather than their fur for insulation and therefore do not suffer from exposure. However, situated at the top of the marine foodchain other pollutants undoubtedly do affect seals. Heavy metals, mercury in particular, occur at high levels in both grey and common seals but without apparent adverse effects. Polychlorinated biphenyls (PCBs) are highly toxic, fat soluble chemicals which have been found at high levels in seal blubber. These by-products of the plastics industry have been linked with reproductive failure and increased rates of disease in grey seals in the Baltic and common seals in Holland and could yet be implicated in the seal epidemic of 1988.

So, although we are fortunate that most of the seas frequented by seals around the British Isles are still relatively unpolluted we cannot afford to become complacent. In contrast to so many other wild creatures, our seals seem to be thriving, but their long term future lies with us. The destruction of the oceans through abuse and neglect could prove to be man's ultimate folly.

During the many hours grey seals *(left)* and common seals *(above)*
spend hauled-out, they only rarely interrupt their apparent
inactivity to scratch or groom.

When about three weeks old, grey seal pups lose their white coats and are left by their mothers to fend for themselves; these 'weaners' then leave the breeding sites and enter the sea for the first time.

Common seal pups, born on intertidal rocks, can swim from birth.

Common seals haul-out throughout the year, often in
large numbers, on sandbanks in the big estuaries on
the east coast of Britain. The most important areas
include those in the Moray Firth and The Wash.

When seen from the air these groups are more widely spaced
than is apparent from the ground.

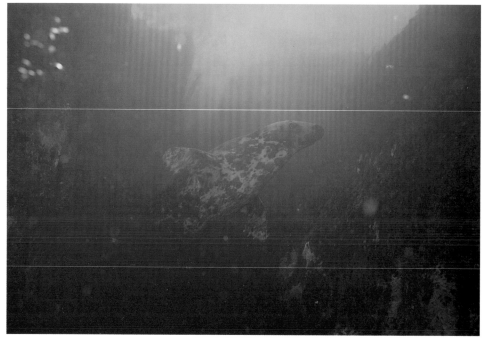

Seals, like this juvenile common seal *(top left)*, are only able to move
around on land with some difficulty. Both common *(above)*
and grey seals *(below left)* are supremely adapted to
life in and beneath the ocean waves.

Seals are predominantly fish-eaters, using their stream-lined bodies
and powerful flippers to pursue their prey and their strong jaws
to catch it. Unfortunately this brings these beautiful and
graceful creatures into deadly conflict with man.

Enjoying Seals

There can be few more enjoyable experiences in the natural world than to sit in a rocky cove on a rare autumn day when the air is still and the sea a tranquil blue. A tumbling raven flies by croaking and the weird, melancholy wail of a grey seal fills the air. It is so strange that when first heard it is difficult to imagine it belongs to this world, more likely the next and with it the realisation that stories of selkies may not be so far-fetched after all. Seals can be frustrating animals to watch – we may only catch a brief glimpse of an inquisitive head which pops up to inspect us or our passing boat, or they appear as little more than specks hauled-out in the distance.

All this changes, however, for those of us lucky enough to dive with them. It is only then, in the seal's own world that we can truly appreciate the graceful beauty of these supremely adapted creatures. The consummate ease with which they twist and turn is a truly humbling experience for the lumbering human diver equipped with sophisticated gear. For those of us keen to see seals at close quarters and not fortunate enough to dive, seal watching trips by boat are probably the best option. These are available at tourist centres on the west coast of Scotland, the Farne Islands and Ramsey and Skomer islands in Wales. At some of these sites you should be able to see both species of seal and so test your powers of observation and identification.

When approaching seals, care should be taken not to cause unnecessary disturbance particularly at breeding sites where this may result in females deserting their pups. It is surely better to view from a safe distance with a pair of binoculars.

Seal Facts

		Common seal	Grey seal
Scientific name		*Phoca vitulina*	*Halichoerus grypus*
Average length -	male	1.5 – 1.8 m	2.0 m
	female	1.2 – 1.8 m	1.8 m
Average weight -	male	80 – 100 kg	230 kg
	female	80 – 100 kg	150 kg
	newborn pup	10 kg	14 kg
Average longevity -	male	20 years	25 years max. 35 years
	female	30 years	35 years max. 46 years
Estimated populations -	UK	25,000	92,000
	world	500,000	215,000
Pupping period in UK		June/July	September-December
Time of moult in UK		July/August	January-March

Recommended Reading

There are several excellent books available which will provide more detailed information either on seals in general or on British seals in particular. These include:

Anderson, S.   *Seals* (1990)   Whittet Books

Bonner, W.N.   *Natural History of Seals* (1990)   Christoper Helm

Thompson, P.M.   *The Common Seal* (1989)   Shire Natural History

Biographical Note

David Miller is a zoologist by training and a conservationist by profession. He is currently the reserve warden on the Isle of Rhum National Nature Reserve off the west coast of Scotland and before that he worked for the University of Aberdeen on a research project investigating the ecology and behaviour of common seals in the Moray Firth, north-east Scotland. He has also worked on other nature reserves with seal populations, including the remote island archipelago of St. Kilda.